THE INVESTMENT MUSEUM

Written by: Spencer Hawthorne Jr.
Illustrated by: Paul Brown

No part of this publication may be reproduced,
stored in a retrieval system,
or transmitted in any form or by any means,
electronic, mechanical, photocopying, recording, or otherwise, without written
permission of the publisher.

For information regarding permission,
email info@jaydensquests.com.
Published by Eight Streams Inc,
by arrangement with IngramSpark.

ISBN: 978-1-7363416-5-0 (HC)
Library of Congress Control Number: 2023900593

Text copyright © 2022 by Eight Streams Inc. Illustrations copyright © 2022 by Eight Streams Inc. All rights reserved.

The publisher does not have any control over and does not assume any responsibility for author or third-party websites or their content.

This is a fictional story All of the characters, names, incidents, organizations, and dialogue in this novel are either the products of the author's imagination or are used fictitiously.

To learn of investments, I had to go see them,
so I took a trip to an investment museum.
What I saw, you just wouldn't believe.
I swear its the truth, I would not deceive.

At the split second as I walked inside, there was a guide standing tall, with a smile stretching wide.

The guide said, "Welcome!!
Please follow me straight,"
and pointed at the sign that read
"INVEST IN REAL ESTATE."

I saw a house flip and twirl all around,
and just as it landed,
money fell to the ground.

I couldn't believe what I had just seen.
How was that investing?
What did that mean?

The guide magically appeared!
Like a rabbit out of a hat,
then whispered in my ear,
"Let's have a little chat."

He said, "Don't look confused,
there's reason to cheer.
I'll explain what you saw,
and make everything clear."

"If you buy a house at a very low price,
and then fix it up to look really nice.
Add TVs, a pool, and even new couches.
When you sell it for a profit,
it's called flipping houses."

Just next door there was a very large crowd,
with high-pitched voices
shouting out loud.

On the way over
the guide showed me a box.
He shouted,
"Hand over all loose items
and hang on to your socks!"

I cut through the line;
there were people in flocks
waiting on the roller coaster
"Investing in Stocks"

This roller coaster was one of a kind.
It soared high,
dipped low,
and rode in a straight line.

Upon our ascent, the crowd started to swell.
On the way down we yelled, "Buy!"
On the way up we screamed, "Sell!"

When the roller coaster ended,
I walked to the guide,
so he could explain
the investing in stocks ride.

He said, "Buy the stocks low,
maybe three or more,
then sell them at a higher price
than what you bought them for."

"The next room is my favorite,
please try to relax."
And just as soon as I entered,
I stopped right in my tracks.

There was a room full of people
all staring at me.
I was shaken to my core,
as shocked as could be.

I thought, this is really weird,
like something you'd never see.
It got weirder when I realized
those people - were actually me.

I looked all around with a curious gaze.
I saw a sign that read,
"Walk Through The Mirror Maze.

I was lost in the maze
with no sense of direction,
yet wowed by what I saw
in my reflection.

At the end of the maze,
I walked to the guide,
so he could explain
what I saw inside

He said, "The other rooms explain
how to generate wealth,
this room shows who you could be
if you invest in yourself."

You have quite some time
before you make that decision,
the mirrors are only there
to give you a vision."

I was learning alot,
wouldn't you know...
The museum was closing soon,
it was time for me to go.

If you can't believe my story,
just know this much is true.
If you learn how money works,
you can make money work for you.

Food for thought:

If Jayden invests in one place,
he could lose everything
if it does not work out.
Jayden could protect himself
by investing in multiple places,
so if one investment doesn't work out
he would still have other options.

Glossary:

401K: an account you get through your job where the money you deposit is invested. Some employers even match the amount you deposit.

Mutual Fund: a way to invest in multiple stocks or bonds at the same time. Example is the S&P 500

Real Estate: investing in real property such as land, homes, and business buildings (also known as commercial buildings).

Invest in Yourself: you can invest your time or money into learning a trade or skill to increase your earning potential.

www.jaydensquests.com

Learn more on quests with Jayden

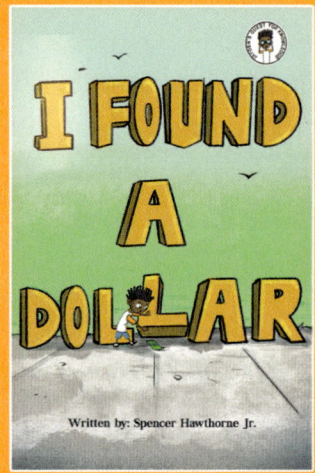

AVAIABLE NOW

FOLLOW US ON SOCIAL MEDIA
@JAYDENSQUESTS

Made in the USA
Middletown, DE
17 January 2025